FROM THE FILMS OF

Harry Potter ™

MAGICAL ART
COLORING BOOK

WIZARDING WORLD

SCHOLASTIC INC.

All rights reserved. Published by Scholastic Inc., *Publishers since 1920*.
SCHOLASTIC and associated logos are trademarks and/or
registered trademarks of Scholastic Inc.

The publisher does not have any control over and does not assume any
responsibility for author or third-party websites or their content.

This book is a work of fiction. Names, characters, places, and incidents
are either the product of the author's imagination or are used fictitiously,
and any resemblance to actual persons, living or dead, business
establishments, events, or locales is entirely coincidental.

ISBN 978-1-338-80000-5

10 9 8 7 6   23 24 25 26
Printed in the U.S.A.   40

First printing 2022

Compiled by Cala Spinner
Select illustrations by Violet Tobacco
Photos @ Shutterstock.com
Book design by Jessica Meltzer

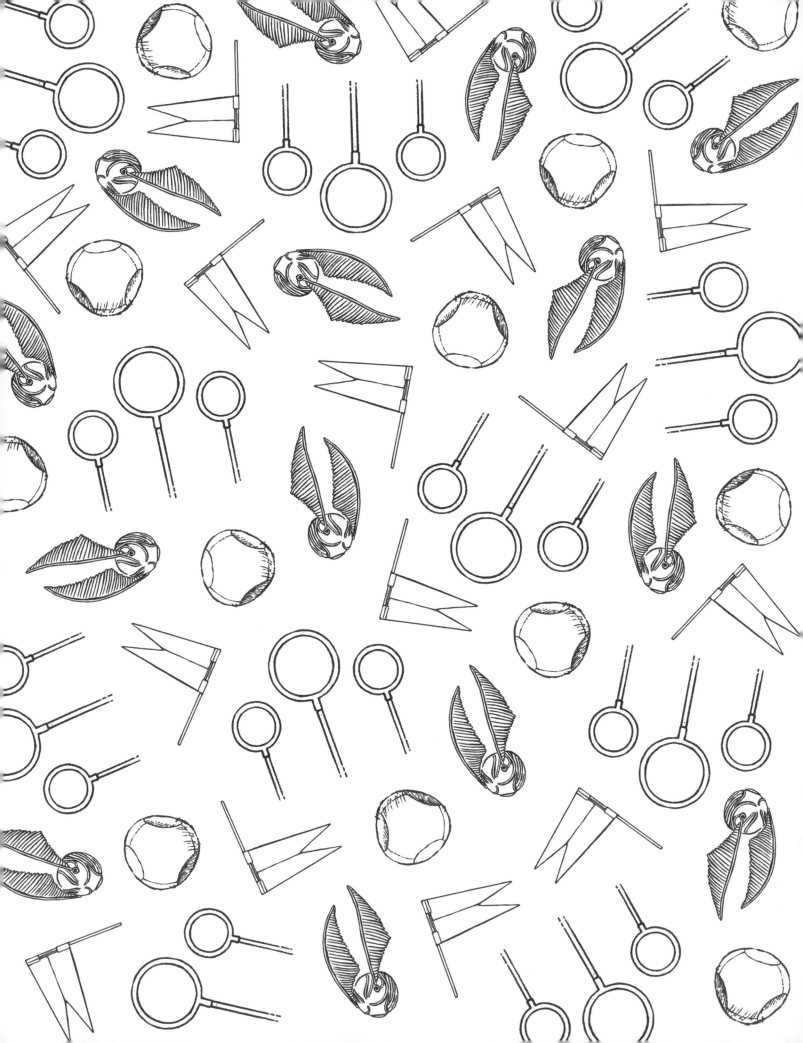

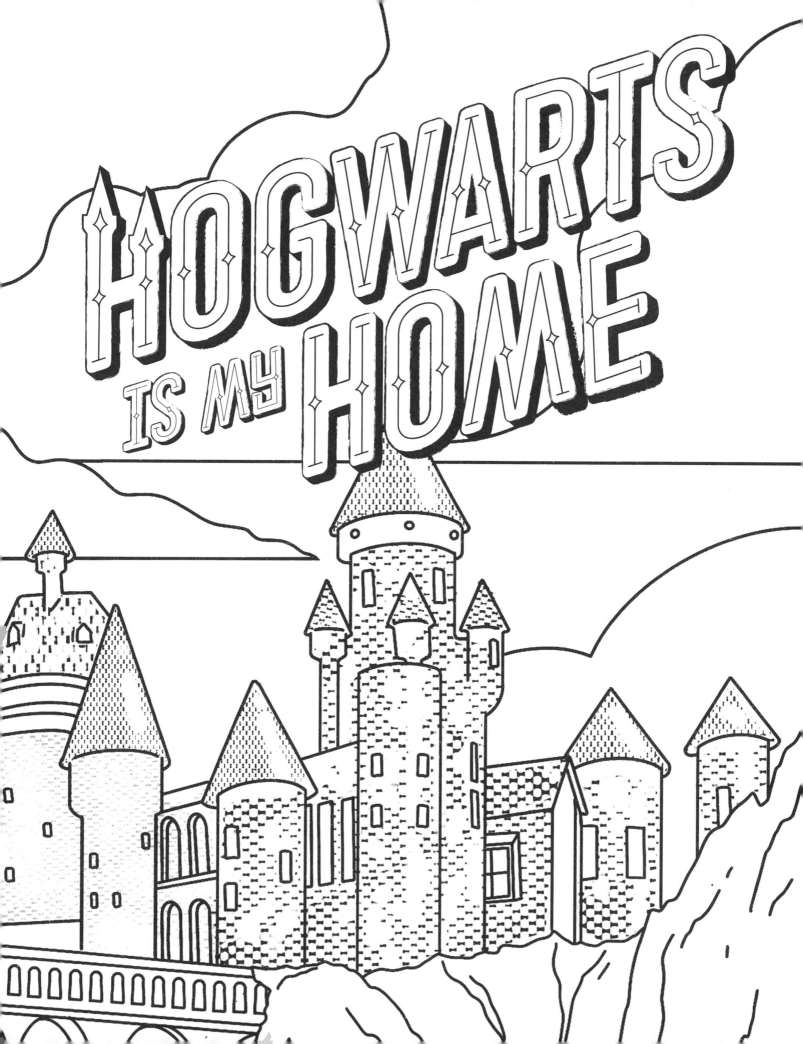

SLYTHERIN™

"I WOULD TRUST HAGRID WITH MY LIFE."

HAPPEE BIRTHDAE HARRY

HAPPEE BIRTHDAE HARRY

"I CHECKED THIS OUT WEEKS AGO FOR A BIT OF LIGHT READING."

"HAS ANYONE SEEN A TOAD? A BOY NAMED NEVILLE HAS LOST ONE."

"THAT WAS BLOODY BRILLIANT!"

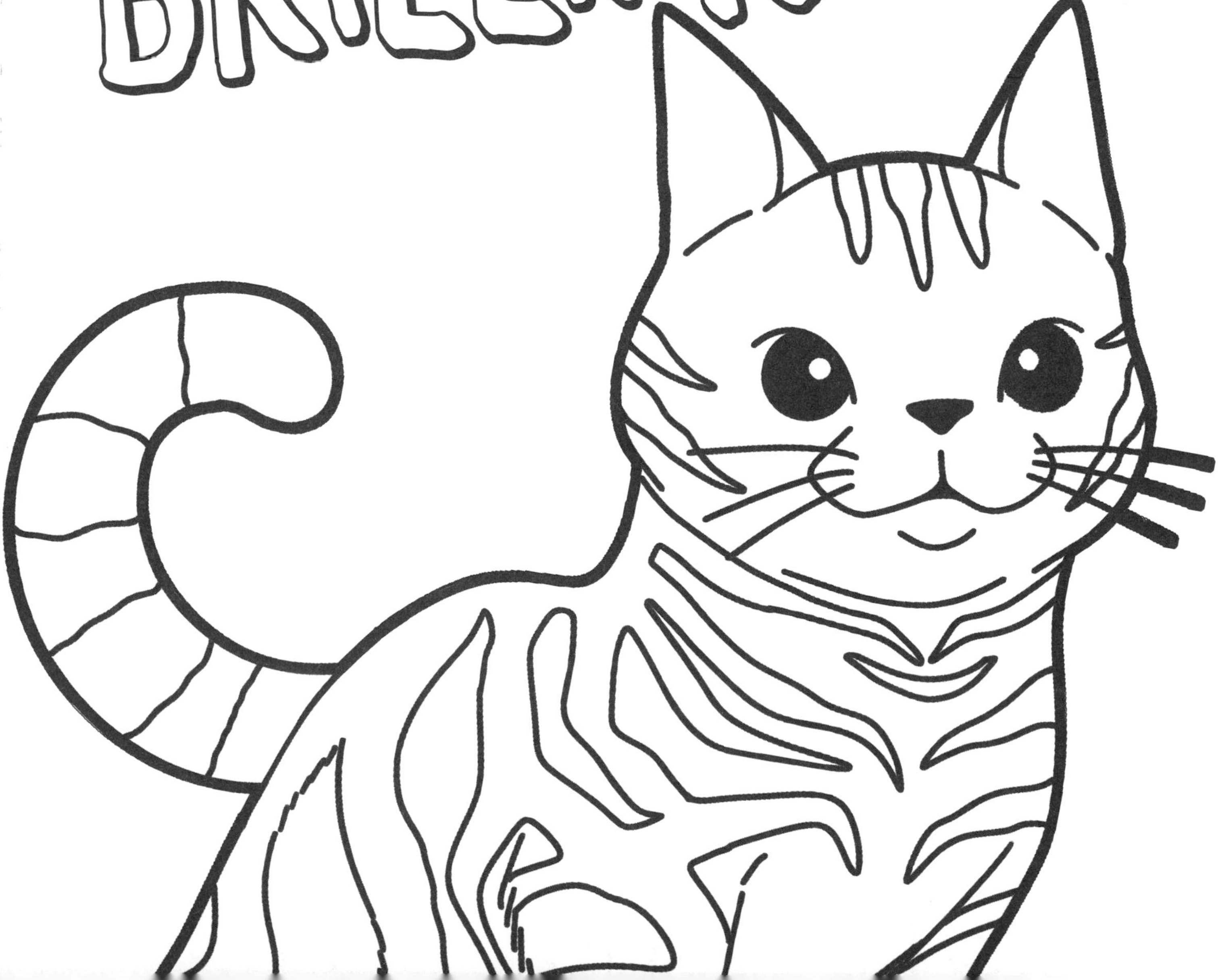

RAVENCLAW™

HUFFLEPUFF™

GRYFFINDOR™

PIGWIDGEON

"YOU NEED US, HARRY."